Beautiful and intensely emotional, memory, love, heartbreak and year

transformative power of the imagination. The Syrian prisons where his poems were written remain places of torture and violence. Yet during his long years of incarceration, the poet captured the elusive bird of freedom in poems smuggled out and published in Beirut and France without his knowledge, words that went on to inspire the Syrian revolution. The impressive collective of translators, writers and critics behind this first collection of Bayrakdar's poetry in English were inspired by Elias Khoury's seminar on Arab prison literature at New York University, and the explosive nature of this literature in a country as closed as Syria. In an interview accompanying the poems, Bayrakdar reveals, "… captivity and freedom … enfold in themselves a charge that does not fade, not for the reader and not for the poet."

> —**Malu Halasa**, co-editor of *Syria Speaks: Art and Culture from the Frontline*, and author of *The Secret Life of Syrian Lingerie: Intimacy and Design*, and *Mother of all Pigs*

Faraj Bayrakdar's poems, written while in prison, are a glorious testament to the power of the imagination and memory. Every page in this magnificent, important book is proof of how "language at the peak of clarity/unfolds the night," how it transcends time and space to create its own kingdom, one where justice and love reign. Those searching for the right words to describe these turbulent days, and to offer hope, will find them here. Bayrakdar is a voice we must listen to, and this is a book that all of us must read.

> **—Maaza Mengiste**, author of *The Shadow King*, shortlisted for the Booker Prize

These searing and open hearted poems, born in prison, scrawled on cigarette paper, smuggled out from Asad's repressive rule in Syria, and now finally translated from Arabic into English, make a fresh contribution to thought as much as to poetry. This thought is conservative in that it protects and preserves a poetics that live on under oppressive conditions. How rare it is to experience pride in being human in contrast to the depravity we have increasingly paraded in public. The prisoner, in mourning for life while that life continues outside, is the keeper of a buried treasure, thought itself and a bit of paper.

> **—Fanny Howe**, poet, novelist and, most recently, author of *Night Philosophy* and *Love and I*

# A DOVE IN FREE FLIGHT

## Faraj Bayrakdar

Edited & Introduced by **Ammiel Alcalay** and **Shareah Taleghani**

Interview with Faraj Bayrakdar by **Muhammad 'Ali al-Atassi**
Portrait of the Poet by **Elias Khoury**

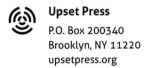

**Upset Press**

P.O. Box 200340
Brooklyn, NY 11220
upsetpress.org

*A Dove in Free Flight*
Published in New York by UpSet Press
Copyright © 2021 by Faraj Bayrakdar

Established in 2000, UpSet Press is an independent press based in Brooklyn. The original impetus of the press was to upset the status quo through literature. UpSet Press has expanded its mission to promote new work by new authors; the first works, or complete works, of established authors—placing a special emphasis on restoring to print new editions of exceptional texts; and first-time translations of works into English. Overall, UpSet Press endeavors to advance authors' innovative visions, and works that engender new directions in literature.

ISBN 978-1-937357-00-9

# A DOVE
## IN
# FREE FLIGHT

### Faraj Bayrakdar

Edited by **Ammiel Alcalay** and **Shareah Taleghani**

Translated by the New York Translation Collective:
**Ammiel Alcalay, Sinan Antoon, Rebecca Johnson,
Elias Khoury, Tsolin Nalbantian, Jeffrey Sacks,**
and **Shareah Taleghani**

# Contents

# Poetry's Migration:

An Introduction to Faraj Bayrakdar's *A Dove in Free Flight*

In a demonstration in liberated Aleppo in the summer of 2013, a protestor held up a sign with the line: "One bird is enough for the sky not to fall." Handwritten and accompanied by a sketch of the three-starred flag of the Syrian Revolution in one corner, these words were taken from the long-form poem, "Mirrors of Absence," written by Faraj Bayrakdar in Saydnaya Prison between 1997 and 2000. As with "Mirrors of Absence," the poems collected here were composed by Bayrakdar while he was still in the midst of a long imprisonment. Like many of those of his generation who opposed the Asad regime, he would endure prison through writing, composing poetry, accessing the creative to sustain himself despite torture, daily degradations, the systemic harsh and annihilating conditions of the Syrian carceral archipelago and security apparatus. Though not everyone was and is able to survive such conditions, like others, Bayrakdar's poetry and other inscriptions would endure incarceration.

Decades before the peaceful protests of the 2011 Revolution and the subsequent war, Faraj Bayrakdar was one of tens of thousands of people imprisoned during and after the period in the late 1970s and early 1980s that is referred to by Syrians simply as *al-ahdath* or "the events" but was termed in English by Middle East Watch, now Human Rights Watch, "the great repression." Various opposition groups, spanning the political spectrum, and including the Communist Action Party of which Bayrakdar was a member, were systematically persecuted by the regime in the wake of armed conflict with factions of the Syrian Muslim Brotherhood which culminated in the massacre of over 1,000 detainees at Tadmor Military Prison in 1980 and the siege and massacre of residents of the city of Hama in 1982, when tens of thousands of people were slaughtered by the Syrian military. Despite these atrocities and vast and lethal mechanisms of silencing perpetrated by the Asad government, many, like Bayrakdar and his comrades, would persist in their opposition and refuse to remain silent. Released in 2000, and still steadfast in his rejection of the Syrian state's despotism, he would eventually be forced to seek asylum in Europe in 2005. He now resides in Sweden where he continues to write, compose poetry, and speak out against the Syrian regime.

To read the poems of *A Dove in Free Flight* is, in one sense, to track the forced itinerary of a Syrian poet and dissident, to trace the effects of his first months of torture and interrogation in Palestine Division (Division 235), his imprisonment in that "kingdom of death and madness," Tadmor Military Prison, and the long years of his detention in the now more infamous Saydnaya. The poems that make up this collection have also had their migrations, traversing barriers and borders long before access to digital publishing was available. Carefully smuggled out of prison by friends, family, and comrades, they traveled from Homs to Beirut, to Paris, and back to Beirut, and then again to Syria. In Paris, they were translated into French, without Bayrakdar's knowledge, by the extraordinary Moroccan poet and former political prisoner Abdellatif Laâbi, in an effort to publicize the case, win support for Bayrakdar, and pressure the Asad regime for his release. Eventually a group of us in New York would read the first Arabic edition and begin the collective translation project that resulted in this book.

That process is a story in itself, and it began in a seminar on "Arab Prison Literature" taught by Lebanese novelist Elias Khoury at New York University in 2002: in other words, after 9/11 and before "shock and awe," the first phase of the US invasion of Iraq in 2003. Members of the seminar, composed of PhD and MA level students, including Shareah Taleghani, and a fellow traveler sitting in on the class, Ammiel Alcalay, formed a tightly knit, politically active, and deeply involved group. Our sense of the enormity of the events just behind us was palpable in our gatherings, whether in or out of class, with so many in the group having direct ties to family and friends in those parts of the world "producing" the news. But the texts we encountered through Elias's extraordinarily intimate and forceful presentation revealed a completely different kind of news, news that had circulated throughout the Arab world for decades and formed the bedrock of political and cultural resistance to despotic regimes.

When we encountered the work and life story of Faraj Bayrakdar, we found that his poems embodied and encompassed all the other more detailed texts we had read; as Bayrakdar himself put it in the interview with Muhammad 'Ali al-Atassi included in our collection:

> The truth is that poetry is the antithesis of prison, just as life is the opposite of death[...] The moment of writing is the moment of true freedom, and poetry is the vastest space of freedom[...] Poetry is democratic with its writer and reader[...] Poetry allowed me to control my prison, rather than my prison controlling me.

Alcalay suggested we translate the collection, *A Dove in Free Flight*, as a group. In addition to us, the present editors of this volume, the group included Sinan Antoon, Rebecca Johnson, Tsolin Nalbantian, and Jeffrey Sacks, with Elias Khoury, thankfully, looking over our collective shoulder. We each took a group of poems and worked on them, sometimes alone and sometimes with one other person or in a group; we then circulated our results so that, somehow, by the end of the process, we'd all had a hand in each translation. We had a somewhat rough but completed manuscript in late Fall of 2002, including Elias's stunning introduction, and we kept tinkering with it. Eventually, in 2004, we began calling ourselves the New York Translation Collective, and our idea was to create a network that could come together on joint projects while developing a new approach to the translation of Arabic texts, emphasizing works that challenged some of the political, aesthetic, and imaginative assumptions and blinders of writers in the United States.

In some sense, our intention was to create the structure of a union, in which translators might gain negotiating power or even veto power since, too often in the US, translations appear without context or history, whether literary or political. In fact, in many instances, writers with less than stellar records might be presented to a largely uninformed public as "dissidents" of one kind or another, with no one being the wiser. Or, even worse, used as cover for US supported regimes and ideologies, deploying all the tools of the cultural-industrial complex to bring certain figures into prominence as a means of erasing others with more significant, conscientious, and courageous histories. As importantly, writers in translation too often jump the line: a heavily derivative younger writer might be presented as a major innovator while the roots of important literary movements and their pioneers remain unknown and un-translated. Our thought was that a collective might present a publisher with demands: if you want this translated, then you have to consider publishing these other texts first. Given that, at the time, not too many people were working as literary translators of Arabic into American English, this wasn't such a far-fetched concept.

As Alcalay wrote in the original 2004 preface, strategic approaches were necessary: "Deprived for so long of direct knowledge from other worlds into American English, there has been somewhat of a bandwagon approach to translation of late. New ventures, many doing enormously useful and worthy work, have emerged. But translation, like any public act, must be strategic to have any effect. There may even be times when NOT translating, withholding certain texts from a public only too ready to consume and discard them, may be one responsible option." It is important, as well, to remember that mainstream approaches to Arabic literature and culture in the US have almost always been subsumed in dominant geo-political considerations and long-standing ideological and historical alliances. Most pioneering work, in the 1960s, 70s, and even into the 1980s, went against the grain, appearing in small presses and rarely garnering much general attention, while anything related to Palestine was suppressed, marginalized, contentious, or made to appear so.

As Alcalay further noted in that 2004 preface: "Only a few years ago the array of Middle East related cultural events now common in New York and the US would have been unthinkable—film festivals, art exhibits, musical performances, theater pieces, poetry readings. This space for cultural expression hasn't come out of a vacuum but is a result of the political consciousness forged through activism focused primarily on the issue of Palestine, the site that still serves as a litmus test for gauging North American political and cultural orientations. One benefit of this new reality is the presence of a diverse group of students studying Arabic literature and a growing interest among the general public to familiarize themselves with things Arabic." It was in this climate that we were working, forging new venues and modes of transmission for Arabic culture. It was also in this climate that Shareah Taleghani, one of those students who is by now part of a cohort of several generations of younger scholars, had the opportunity to go to Syria in 2005 to meet with Faraj and study his revised and corrected manuscript together in detail, particularly since the

18

original edition we had been working from had been published without Faraj's knowledge or involvement in the final editing process.

Between 2003 and 2005, a number of our group's translations appeared: in *Beyond Baroque* magazine, the on-line translation journal *Words Without Borders*, the venerable UK based *Banipal*, the longest standing magazine continually devoted to Arabic literature in English translation, and *BOMB* magazine, a mainstay of the US avant-garde. In other words, a variety of audiences began to get exposed to Bayrakdar's powerful work, and each appearance provided at least a brief summary of the complex circumstances in which the poems had been written. By 2006, the book was prepared for publication under the Beyond Baroque imprint, edited by Fred Dewey, but blowback from a neo-con attack on Alcalay led to funding issues and the project became unsustainable. From that point on, in other words, for fourteen years, from 2006 until 2020, when UpSet Press agreed to publish *A Dove in Free Flight*, numerous publishers were approached and no one saw fit to publish the collection, even during the revolutionary promise initiated in 2011 and the ensuing horrors that came, for a while, to dominate the selective coverage of the mainstream media.

But even that old standby to pique US readership and literary interest—catastrophic war and civilian carnage—did not suffice in this case. Without daring to make any comparisons, one cannot help but at least make the analogy: Faraj Bayrakdar was in prison roughly the same time it took to find a

US publisher for his work. Beyond the particular circumstances of any one publisher, this process, we would hope, ought to be recognized for what it is: an alarming instance of public intellectual, artistic, and political erasure, and yet another way in which vital information—the actual lifeblood of a besieged but still breathing world—is withheld from the US public.

This is even more striking given that Bayrakdar's work is a document of rare integrity and primary human import—his ability to describe and differentiate the role of poetry and the character of each individual in relation to their actions and not their ideology is a source we should pay close attention to and humble ourselves before, especially now, as attempts to hijack just grievances by political opportunism seeps into the most intimate areas of our lives, threatening to crumble even the possibility of political thought and action. Like so many that have come before him to bear witness, Bayrakdar has borne the burden of the utmost in human depravity, only to emerge through the voice of poetry.

In Bayrakdar's responses to Muhammed 'Ali al-Atassi, there is a theory, a method, and a philosophy of being intimately entwined in the poetic act, and we ignore what Bayrakdar has to impart at our own peril. His thought and his poems denote and describe an absolute rift that enable us to embrace the past as if we had never known it, with an emotional validity that is profound and unquestionable. As we come to an end point in the consumption of generalized and mediated terminology, Bayrakdar's clarity and profundity is startling. In speaking about his body during imprisonment and torture, he says: "Luckily, my body never abandoned me, and consequently, periods of time passed in which I began to commiserate with it and apologize to it. In a way, I am also responsible for its torment. My love for my body was great, especially in the initial period of interrogation. It is my most loyal friend, and even while it complains to me sometimes, not to weaken or abandon me, but so that I commiserate with it—I felt towards it like the way Antara felt towards his horse."

It is here where, if we leave aside the geographical journeys of the texts and the poet himself and the traces of a prison lexicon (the cell, the tower, the hunger strike) intertwined in some of the verses, we also find in Bayrakdar's poetry the powerful and poignant resonances of the classical poetic heritage with gestures towards the motifs of the pre-Islamic qasidas and the defiance and rebellion of the Sa'alik, or brigand poets, as well as the echoes of Sufi masters. The past reopens before us, like something we can sift in our hands.

What then does it mean to read these poems that Faraj Bayrakdar composed and refined over the course of thirteen years, seven months, and seventeen days in prison more than twenty years ago? Reading, like translation, can be, at the very least, a gesture of solidarity, but solidarity in a US context has itself become a contested issue. In the rush to confront the catastrophic nature of US regime change policies, too many commentators and intellectuals have themselves succumbed to the dictates of propaganda, in which only one clear-cut position is admissible in public. This has largely been the case with Syria, and the idea that one can (and must) express solidarity with citizens and survivors of brutal regimes and their confrontations with oppression while holding onto more nuanced political positions is too rarely expressed or even imagined.

To read *A Dove in Free Flight* in the wake of the Syrian Revolution is to be reminded of the connections between those who rose up against the Syrian state in peaceful protests in March 2011 in Dar'a, Homs, Hama, Idlib, Aleppo, Ghouta, and Douma, and countless cities across the country and those from earlier generations, like Bayrakdar, who directly opposed the Asad regime, at times paying the highest possible price. And yet, like the revolutionaries and protestors chanting first in 2011 and renewed, in Suweida in 2020, Bayrakdar's poetry is ultimately a steadfast rejection of despair and political apathy, a reminder that "one bird is enough for the sky not to fall." Even in the face of a relentless politics of cruelty, it is still possible for the poet to say:

And so that the sky will not be confined
I'll release a flock of stray doves
and open the towers of my spirit for the day to come.

*Ammiel Alcalay and Shareah Taleghani*

# Portrait of a Poet

At New York University where I taught a seminar on the prison in contemporary Arabic literature, I discovered, through a number of modern Arabic fictional and poetic texts, that the prison forms a basic trope in Arabic writing. In fictional texts of Abdelrahman Munif, Sonallah Ibrahim, Fadhil al-'Azzawi, Bensalem Himmich, Naguib Mahfouz, and Gamal al-Ghitani among others, the prison takes on the mirror image of writing. Prison produces a literary approach that searches for writing and/or emancipation through writing. The literature engages in its own approach to the relationship of the experience of prison. It also establishes a balance between the desire for freedom and a writing that resembles a tattoo in its ability to engrave for itself a place in the body of the language. Literary Arabic writing is tattooed by prison. Perhaps the title that the Iraqi Abdelrahman al-Majid al-Rabi'i chose for the novel about his experience in prison—*The Tattoo*—is the greatest indication of the deep wound that oppression and dictatorship have inscribed on the body of contemporary Arabic literature.

Among the tales and the tortured souls, a small collection of poems by the Syrian poet Faraj Bayrakdar made us pause; *A Dove in Free Flight* is a collection which the poet wrote during his long incarceration in Syrian prisons. His friends published it in Beirut without his knowledge so that the book could become one of the instruments of pressure on the authorities of his country and mobilize international, intellectual opinion, particularly in France, for the purpose of setting the poet free.

Both the interview with the poet that was published by Muhammad 'Ali al-Atassi in the cultural supplement of Beirut's daily *al-Nahar*, and the poems which abound with a dream and a despair made our readings of the poems a personal experience for each of us. The students chose poems in order to translate them into English. Through my attempts to help them fathom meanings and connotations, I discovered that the poetry—as the whisper of a language that approaches the terror of silence and eliminates the barriers between languages—was able to address the different levels of our consciousness and unconsciousness.

The poet wrote his poems with ink made from tea and onion peels using a thin wooden stick in place of a pen. From prison to prison and torture to torture, he takes us on his voyage to experience the connection between the body and the soul. The body is annihilated under the beatings or the electric shock or the "tire" or what has no end in the dictionary of Arab oppression whereas the soul protects, commiserates with, and shelters the body. This relationship resembles that of memory to writing; memory protected from oblivion the poems that Bayrakdar could not write down in Tadmor Prison. And when writing did come in Saydnaya Prison through ink that was not ink, it allowed memory to be liberated from the need for recollection and opened up the possibilities of forgetting.

In his prison, the poet appropriates all of Arabic poetry. It is as if he has granted his experience to a collective memory crafted from the images, rhythms, and forms accumulated in the Arabic language. Thus, we come across the tension of the language intertwined with the symbol as in the poetry of Darwish. Yet we also find Malik Bin al-Rayb as he attempts the echo of the dualism of Imru al-Qays who introduced tragedy into pre-Islamic poetry. When Imru al-Qays resorted to the dual form, he addressed his divided self as two halves—one half for mourning and the other for love. But when Bayrakdar further divided this dual form, he was searching for the soul that had been separated from both its own despair and the body that protected it from ruin.

Faraj Bayrakdar mingles love with poetry and despair with sorrow. He presents a personal experience about the story of an individual confronting terror and death. One becomes divided in order to merge others with his fragmentation, and the poet resorts to imagery of women and a daughter in order to reveal his body as a solitary, locked cell.

Faraj was arrested for the first time in 1978 for a period of three months because, along with comrades, including the late short story writer Jamil Hatmal, he published a small journal called "The Literary Notebooks." Yet his journey in prisons began in 1987 with the accusation of political activities through his association with a small leftist party, the Communist Action Party in Syria. In the three prisons to which he was transferred—Palestine Division, then the horrifying Tadmor, and finally Saydnaya—the poet traversed a purgatory of sorrow, loneliness, and pain. He returned to poetry to retrieve the air that his lungs had lost; in Tadmor, he wrote the poems in his memory, and in Saydnaya, he recorded them and sent them to the outside. He discovered that poetry is not an articulation of experience but rather that poetry, itself, is an experience that grants the prisoner his freedom inside the damp, desolate cells.

In his poem "Hunger Strike," he reveals himself as a tree:

> In the last part of night
> of blood and memory
> in the last neigh
> > of empty stomachs
> the human tree reveals
> > its prophecy
> > > and pours forth our meager
> > > > stature

In his poem "Neighing," he discovers the relationship between the body and freedom:

> for my prison cell is my body
> and the ode incidental freedom

And then he takes us to a combination of passion and sorrow:

> The blue of depth is sadness
> and the depth of blue—sadness
> and we are nothing but it.
> Are we in its mirror,
>            or is it in ours?

Faraj's journey has been long and difficult: for in his search for his threatened life and existence, he fashioned a personal song for freedom. The prisoner, himself, becomes a story because the prisoners' freedom of expression and opinion in the Arab world becomes the only liberty in a time of oppression, dictatorship, and the absence of civil society.

A poet has given us words emanating from pain; his words proceed forward and then stumble resembling the embers of a scream of resistance combined with a cry for help:

> I cry out
> I am not searching for a collective grave
> Just my country

When will the country hear you, poet? And when will the grave no longer be the only remaining space of the nation?

*Elias Khoury*
*2002*

*Translated by Shareah Taleghani*

A Dove in Free Flight

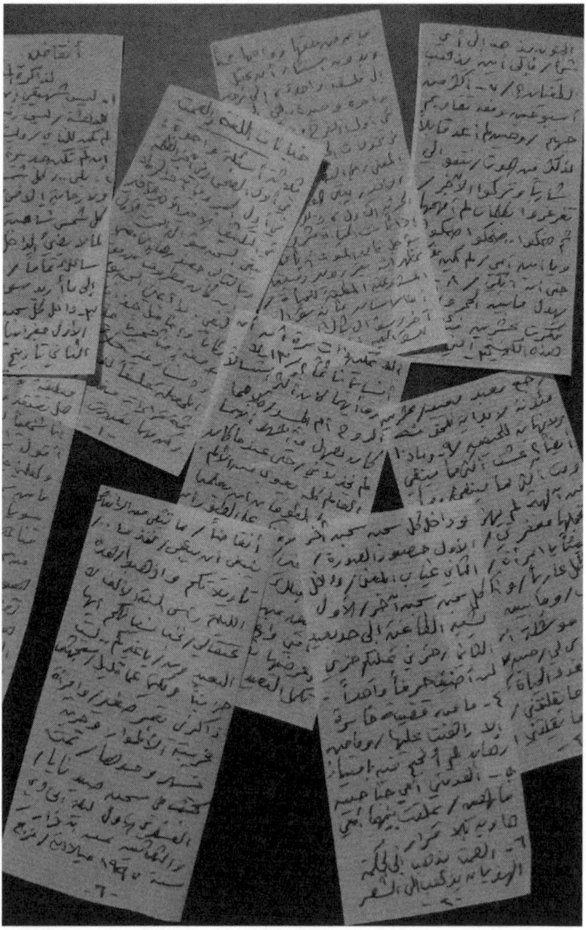

The freedom within us is more powerful
than the prisons we are in.

—*Faraj*

## Two Verses

She doesn't flutter like any butterfly
      to stir  his heart like a
              pomegranate blossom —
It's no one but him — so does he say to her:
Enough of your blue butterfly —
Enough of my craving to
          be shoreless!

    *    *    *

Shadow rests on the trees
         and memories on hard labor.
Neither are you the ruins for which I cry
nor are the poets like me when they mourn.
The wind has cloaked me
after passing through the wheat:
wind — mistress of the fields
wind — mistress of the horses
wind — mistress of the reeds.

    *    *    *

She doesn't coo like any dove
moistening the sky —
oh god, my wife!
oh god, our daughter!

oh god, two fugitive gazelles
    kiss my soul with two verses of dew
    and race on.
Oh lightning,
    shadow their steps —
Horizon,
take my heart and embrace them
so the deluge/might be delayed.

*Damascus/Palestine Division 1987*

# Story

Once upon a time.
Epoch son of time
                told me.
That fire is a guide
so make sure you've got enough
for a long and rugged ride.


            *    *    *


Attempt night anyway
And if despair knocks the door
                        upon you,
no matter —
Rise up
                and write on the walls
without explication or detail:
Oh Master Despair,
        tell your Lord the Sultan
that the cell is no narrower
        than his grave
that the cell is no shorter
        than his life —
This —

If the earth accepts his corpse,
enclosed by footsteps,
and protected by forgetfulness.

*Palestine Division April 1987*

# Cooing

Your cooing wears me out at night.
        So wear me out.
Like wine in the odes, you go on cooing
and leave me what moves horses
            to tears,
what weighs birds down with more wings
what singing follows.
Your coo is a cradle
                kept from rocking
     cornered by absence.
Is the tree of the heart enough
if our wind was shattered
and we too were shattered with the wind?
Is the tree of the heart made of our blood,
       or mirage?
A question seduces me shooting star by shooting star
       a flower a flower or two
numb upon my arm
    as dawn steals blue
to bathe the dew
      so I see it.


And for this question, the gazelle,
     and what binds us
in the nets of the answer
 — and so the sky won't be confined —

I'll release a flock of stray doves
and open the towers of my spirit for
                    the day to come —
So if your cooing drowns me,
        let me drown —
and if you wake me up
I'll leave a crack of dream open
                        and sleep.

*Palestine Division 1987*

# Howl

No one but us
        a corpse hanging... the coming day,
                    and me.
Nor is the city a mother
                  bringing my long death to an end
              nor a star for me to become her son.
Who is at the door?
Do you have my corpse?
I don't *hear* you well!
        All right, all right,
it is...
Maybe it's the student's carcass
                  passing beyond us.


The wind was a noose —
        heaven indifferent,
                and the river...
Who is knocking at the door?
We haven't been here
your last thousand ruins.
Dread has sealed the last window
in the mountain's calm.


I said I was leaning my back
        on a stone or a wall
And there was nothing but the plains

I'll just howl then —
many a wolf on the plain  hears me
and answers.
But first let us cry together —
Wolf, oh Wolf, cry with me again:
earth isn't a prison cell
but you are solitary and bereft
and I, I have no blue bird —
it has yet to fall down between us!
That day—there was nothing, my friend,
just a corpse hanging
the coming day...
a corpse —
and me.

# A Poetic Proximity to Dancing

Yes...
He, alone, exhumes the spirit
extracts it from its corporeal dungeons
even if it arrives in its bareness —
Shooting stars are its likeness
showering down in a void of conditions
to stipulate the absolute.
Well, yes...
You've been disappeared from his presence
so you envision him
sitting upon the glory of thrones —
No one but him shall awaken the Earth
and no secret is more clear:
that he is the singular-enigmatic confounds me
I testify fallacy
        is a believer with him
and then I testify
that the birds are his cells —
who alone is all of this but him
I call to him from the edge of the universe:
Are you the nation of the river?
So the unknown is scorned —
or a flock of goats:
if they bolted, would I not have a body?
It's as if the stars are your fragments
and my wife gathers them every now and then

like she gathered me.
I'm entering into you
    so the mirage will be
I'm leaving you
    so I can see you without borders
Oh, absolute antithesis
absolute pledge —
I face you as a way out
and leave my heart to the wilding
    and my doubt to the fire
I face you as a way out
and leave his estrangement and my extinction to the sea
I face you as a way out
and leave the discovery of
the poem to my friends.

# Vision

I imagined myself weak
my friend Malik Bin al-Rayb
greeted me and gave me sanctuary.
I was neither alive
nor dead so I made room for him
oh, how the tightness of the space shamed me.
I was destroyed
borne on the final wound or stone
I was cloaked in my blood and my love.
I said: would you allow me
a verse in your one elegy, Malik?
for death is a coward
and I am sorrow to a sorrow
and within me is what makes death lonely
even with the dead
so he said:
I remember those who are mourning you
and I was told
other than us there are many
and the clouds are few
and if you and the banners are a tinted horizon
the sun veers toward it and it leans
truly she speaks softly to you
a river or a star
or an eagle its broken wings both a vision and ruin
for you all people are

distress and determination
and everything impossible except you is transformed
the struggle between you and fate is as strong
as the horse's neighing and promised embrace

*Palestine Division April 1987*

# Hunger Strike

In the last part of night
of blood and memory
in the last neigh
        of empty stomachs
the human tree reveals
     its prophecy
           and pours forth our meager
               stature.

*Tadmor Prison 1989*

# Neighing

Stop, and weep

Not sadness over the corpse of
the remnants of a distant god
and so not a sadness
over a bird burdened with open space
Don't take me —
Don't leave me —
maybe, my two friends,  it's a wasteland without language
maybe you both can postpone the probability of death a little
for my prison cell is my body
and the ode incidental freedom.

                *    *    *

A palm tree shakes off its pollen
breaking into tears —
Whom have I struck,
if the lightning-herder goes astray?
And who has struck me?
Is he rising?
The earth follows —
is he falling?
Overcome,
surely he is higher than the sky below.

*    *    *

I said this is my vision
and my bleeding attests to it
The river doesn't bend except
for this wager.
But I, when a woman falls heavily
at the end of night, I forget my hands
on her voice, and then she slips away
leaving me my chains,
to write something, finally —
But I, whenever within me
the late birds struggle
the horizon chokes
or has the hour's mirage
raised the dust I gargle?
Oh, these two...
give me back a little space
since my cell is a body I claim
and a freedom that claims me —
Give me back a question
for the answers scattered by the tribes
or that scattered me over them,
no harm in that...
The coming day, overflowing, will gather me
teardrop by teardrop, like an ode in its cradle,
and then illuminate me suddenly,
like a verse at its climax,
and bless me with its antithesis.

\*    \*    \*

Oh sister
Oh mother
Oh any lover
If god saw his image
in our embraces, it would be revealed
But he doesn't see —
other than locked doors
and shackles —
And the sky stretches
under the soldiers' boots —
other than a braided sky
its throne is of blood
its law acid —
Does the spirit breathe in
from the trees of Dujayl,
the description and the bombardment making them stagger
until they send back what's been inhaled as blood in Rabat?
That minaret — a stab in the void
That mast — its heel in dirt
that doesn't end in the sky.

This is Golgotha
and blood washes the Nile
of its water,
Barada of its nightmares,
and the Euphrates.

*   *   *

I said this is my vision
and you, both, witness
an ember... two embers... three
And dawn breaks
its blue doesn't stray
neighing, neighing
running its course
making known the parting of this time —
We're all heading toward what's to come
They've all passed on to what's gone.
So cushion me in the tenderness of my wounds then,
and get up
The child writes in the "sea" meter
at the beginning of his notebook:
And they stand — only a step —
shedding just a tear
as they get up.

*Tadmor Prison 1992*

# Ode of Sorrow

The blue of depth is sadness
and the depth of  blue — sadness
and a star quivering tears in this space —
Language at the peak of clarity
unfurls the night
to finish the questioning.
The moment is wounded by the dream and departs
burdened by the prophets
and the neighing of memories to come.

                *    *    *

The blue of depth is sadness
and the depth of blue — sadness
and  we are nothing but it.
Are *we* in its mirror,
                or is *it* in ours?
all the same...
The silence of my woman is salt on
        my voice, bearing the meaning
of the wound, and the name of the river,
but her hands are my two shores.
        Her silence is the foot of a turquoise mountain —
How my voice assassinates me at night in its
        direction to prayer and recants a martyr
to witness what I don't see!

        Twilight of rose
that forgetfulness wounds — this sadness
my mother is its mother
wind at the last flute
spelling the river so we can run —
its willow the child flowing after us
        like an echo of the call to prayer.
Oh, mother, I said:
— who between us is sadder
        you or the river or the lightning
        between my hands?
She whispered to me
folding me upon
                a moist eyelash:
— After us comes the dove
— After us?
My voice colored her,
holding the moon back from its time,
two skies bent over in the palms of her hands,
and she urged: Oh, my son,
Sadness began its
        first names with us and overflowed
since the desert —
                Sand hangs loosely over the memory
and a memory hangs the black
over the humble white
and the white over the widespread black
to watch over embers by the ashes
since trees inscribed poetry and life

in the land's copy book —
Indeed, from exile to exile —
in between which commentaries on the country have grown longer
since the blood of an East split

     to present us Damascus.
And so we summarize the wheat and the wisdom.
Two lines slowly

     we return creation to the beginning,
not to sleep.


     \*    \*    \*


Which spirit
flutters this night in the sails of
the infinite, or over its masts?
The sand grouse has passed into thought
God passes in sadness,

      a distant woman passes,
silence and meaning pass,

     and a sail already passed  announcing
the journey on a rainy day.
Oh, this soil...

     who reckons my thoughts?
My daughter's two eyes echo the
trilling cries of joy at evening.
And a sash of the recitation of clouds —
she can awaken vision
and tears in the eyes of the blind.

She lowers eyelashes more savory
than slumber stealing the bird
between its wings,
and a heart from the hands of my mother,
and  shackles from my hands
She resolved the dream's intention:
sadness smiling a little —
she saw a mother —
        the past falling apart in her wake
and a father, his restitution worn away by ruins
        This — his night confounds
        the stars — six gallows
        from which a tree,
                horses, and odes dangle.
Oh, this soil — who but you
begins other than at the end!
Captivity is this which
your spirit conceals... and the spring
the lover bathes in
And the distant Iraqi voice.
Captivity, the shadow
pouring it forth softly, glows.
This is what the likely captive said —
He saw me casting lots and went on:
— Has the hand of sadness
                knocked at your door?
                He unravelled the noose
from memory that shone like silver:
This is my woman, my sorrow —

How often does she come?
How often do I go to it?
Its night is the lightning that awakens
the secrets of prophecies and recites
                    them like rain —
it was in the beginning and we were it
So name *it*, then, the playing of music,
        and name *me* string.
I said, you are still on the bank
and the river is flowing.
Be with the river and see the sadness
as God sees it.
        His mother is distant behind the balconies
Like a tree discovering the wind
        and digging deep into the soul's soil.
Its cup forgiveness, as far as it goes,
        and the flood, insofar as it can,
and poetry its echo.


Its cup is the rain of the inside,
until sinner and saint are equal
in this attire
and the volcano offers him a toast
for the final escape.


*Tadmor Prison 1992*

# An Alphabetical Formation

*Alif*

You're not beginning
This is a blazing eternity
I mean a pulsing ever-after
I mean we are their shadow in the water
Do you see what I see?
Do you roam in the clamor like a lover
Favored by the wind
And here you are the coming day
Raise your cavalry behind the invisible
but don't abandon the horizon or the sea or the soil
lines for beginnings
finish me off at your ease
      You are not beginning now
Watch out...
      anyone who begins gets taken in.

*Ba*

We haven't yet finished an elegy for the century,
      We haven't exposed  blood,
      flowing from poetry,
or a tear from prose,
and there aren't any windows
      through which to see them, the others

and the others are us
Do the dead epitomize the living?
Well, then... does captivity test the
wings a bird uses to
        swoop  down freely,
finding no meaning that isn't
        far from their twin meanings?


*Ta*


That's a mirror,
        and this a woman,
the woman rises
So let the mirror be shattered, and the ruler,
        and the secret between them
The woman rises
        to see the before and the after
from the inside and the outside
We have disregarded the sky
        and performed ablutions upon rising,
then prayed at its knee until noon
the sultans passed by without their dreams,
they were dragging coffins
we call thrones!
Do we really see?... We ask ourselves —
How is it they've triumphed?
Only defeat has been victorious.

*Kha*

The beginning of wine is the shadow
      And it isn't content with the volcano,
      we've raked the languages of serenity,
          to raise
a glass the naked trees/our remains
For he who gathers enough
of the silence that extinguishes an ember
      we no longer grasp, we've returned
      and raked letters
      whose eyes have lost their lashes in sorrow,
for a glorious silence
      they have pierced its seclusion...
the silence indicts armies
and judges... and turncoats... and titles
It doesn't forget. So discard it from your master's resolutions
      and from the binding ties that remind.

*Thal*

This coming day, oblivious of intent
and yesterday breathes in
of our first humanity
oblivious, even, of our first blood.
The lilac is embodied in its meaning
and is there no meaning to the lilac
without us?
What longing cleanses the vision of awareness?

I am the step that wounds the wasteland
and I am the wind with no saddle
and my dreams a dove
Whenever I dispatched it, it declared a sky
for you to sleep in its shadow, my daughter, until my return
I haven't yet said my question
I have said but my shadows
I have said but a grievous anthem
that did and still does resist.

*Nun*

A palm tree is my rib
And my spirit a brown horse
And memory my pavilion
To whom do I leave my belongings?
And to whom do I entrust my desire
for a mirage that doesn't betray its master
      one day as the capitols
      have betrayed their inhabitants.

*Yah*

Has he finished?
No...
He doesn't know this verb,
and doesn't accept its conjugations,
it embarks within us...
and if he arrives to shore,
he says: Apologize to it for me

      Around me is a vaster blueness

      out of your dreams

      Imru al-Qays

            was straying from it

            and so, it strayed from him.

The poet has finished, and as for the poetry

We say: No

And we say: we'll try.

*Saydnaya Prison 1992*

# A Visit

Finally —
unlike what hadn't been usual for him —
my darling smiled at her name.
The universe celebrated by adding two extra skies
                                        and butterflies
wore wings
                of pure freedom.
Thanks, said the forests
            as they combed their hair with the wind.
Thanks, said the seagulls
as they shook
            the fatigue of the first migrations
off their wings.
Thanks, said the waves
as they performed their dance
            on an oceanic altar of passion.
Wheat fields stirred
            and dreams tamed the storms
            and God retook his throne again.

Finally —
and like what had been usual till then,
the guard's voice gurgled
            making known the end of the visit

the prison grilles close her
                    eyes
and the walls don
a hue of deep shame.

*Saydnaya Prison January 26, 1993*

# Portrait

The curse said to him be

                              so he was.

His eyes two dirty copper buttons

his nose an exclamation point

        drawn viciously.

His mouth the shape of a silencer

and his tongue in the barrel of the gun.

On his shoulders peacocks rest

bloated with defeats

he owes debts that would

bankrupt even the blood banks —

He tends to us

with a blind heart

and guards us

with barbed wire

his intentions are booby-traps

        and his smile heralds a massacre.

His wisdom is death

        and his justice hell.

Forgive me... I'll stop.

I'm about to faint —

Maybe he's not exactly like that —

Yet,

he is...

*Saydnaya Prison February 1993*

# Groans

\*     \*     \*

Here I am you alone
in this mad, gaping blindness.
Here I am you alone and death all together
with the predators and the seers and the informers
Maybe I've come to
the very end of my tether
for you to come to the last
dream.
Flare up until you see me and
become complete until I see you.
My rose between two fires
inflaming me
so I might incite wisdom
in this ruin.
I have tried
to the end of the flower and the fire —
how, then, have they isolated my voice
and your silence?
Have you leaned on a belated sword?
Or have you been exchanged — one absence for another?!

\*     \*     \*

Here I am you alone — what are you but I —
I was not before me but you *were* after you.

The shadow has shed the blood of the sun
on the horizon and the night has hissed —
the night has hissed
How late you are... how you've changed...
And you would not be laid bare  — Take no offense from me —
You have your shrouds.


\*      \*      \*


With thorns the guard caresses
your sparrows
and the state bestows upon you
a precautionary death
and enough of the darkness
for you to go  — so go.
You are aware of the insanity of death
thus the music breaks out
and your myths are shaken —
This other body is in the square:
Are you asking me
who splattered the name of God
and the throne with blood?
No time...
This other body —
Who will take it from me
and who will take me from it?
And who testifies that death
has grown weary?
The obscure caresses your vacancies
with wires and blasphemy

I have tried often
as the constellation has mourned the horizon of a poem
I said I have tried often
and with lilac, I have caressed
your night.

\*     \*     \*

The river has been choked with the tears of a woman
whose son was
more pure than she had hoped for
but her dreams were fractured in the night.
God was in a seventh slumber,
as was her son
For who would disturb him
before the dawn call to prayer?
And who, Sister,
now bestows upon you
a palm of his stature
a cloud of his laughter
a breadth of his hands?
The river has been choked with the tears of a woman —
she resembles my mother
just as you resemble me
and now you are alone.

\*     \*     \*

Extinction has escaped you
Let the night shed light on you

and the blossoms darken —
And the wind has enfolded you —
how the wilderness prays for you
And forgetfulness has been hailed.
To where
shall I proceed with your pledges?
I am not asking about places
my prison is a place,
except that the times
have been divested of the right
to travel freely and of
the right of place.
Seven clouds and your memory
have withered in my coat.
Are you mourning?
The salt of your tears and the poet is
in the reach of his poem.
He writes it —
Or let me say: it writes him
Or both write:
Perhaps you are bringing me flowers
But tell me...
after you, who will bring *you* flowers
Our night brings its elegy  to the surface
on the long "sea" meter
I see my face above the wave
or is that
your face?
The salt of your tears —

so permit me to
Close my eyes a little
A little
And a little.
I have not yet handed over my directions
to the judgment of the sand.
Behind me a time
ashamed of the deceits of geography.
Thanks to the sparrow
that built a nest on the other
window and flew.
Breaker of my back
your shadow is now a burning tomorrow
upon whose line I hang my rain
and call to you with what's in the spirit
from the horse's groan —
Do you hear me?
I am calling:
I'm not searching for a collective grave...
Just my country.

*Saydnaya Prison February 1993*

# This Is Him Now

*(to Muhammad 'Abbud, with all his names)*


What an elegy —
when his body is his spear
and his wings a flock of birds.

This is the blood of my shore
so don't shutter the balconies
This is a tireless morning
knocking at the prison cells...

Which elegy,
when his body is a spear
and his wings a flock of birds?

This is the blood of my shore
so don't shutter the balconies
and this is a tireless morning
knocking at the prison cells...

A torrent of horses race
to the precinct of the heart
And the night lets open its white shrouds
Water is the secret of this mirage
And in its blood, an abundant star
and plains of wheat without end
and two communal hands.

Take him to his next day like a palm tree
Read what is left of him
He is the Holy Book struck by rain deferred
Oh absolute wretched one, what will you instigate?
And his body is his river when he runs
And his body is a road in this country
Indeed...
The earth begins with a road
The sea begins with a wave
And the heavens with the polar star —
This is him now...
His mirror has no fixed horizon
And his eyes grow wider and wider.

Oh plain, bring back your yield
Pass by the village in the the attire of the slain.
A meteor has fallen from our galaxy
A triumphal arch bowed at his feet
and revived him with the brightness of gulls
How they uttered the words:
"His intentions are my wings"
Then they flew.
And the schoolgirls greeted him: "Peace"
So he extended his hand to the students
and gave them red stripes
from the flag he was wearing
and they flew...
And the north wind rapped on the door
and the newspaper

and the mailman
the hands of his mother and comrades
And he flew...
Yet, he still congregates among us:
So read a body riddled with wounds
every wound a manifesto.

# Creation

\*　　\*　　\*

She left a waist in the wind and
two hands.
I wasn't a flute before
the wings of birds weren't
And who knows that the sea
is a cry in the beginning
overflowing with lovers
who parted at a teardrop the drop
murmuring with a rainbow when they met
And at night the depth of the moment is an eye.

\*　　\*　　\*

She left a scarf in the wind
        and a field of reed
You, like a kid, fleeing towards forty
love goes but finished where it began
and fatigue passes to its own end.
I was told… I don't remember,
or I remember but I was told
that she rested my head, a trembling dove at first light
and even if the shore weren't shaded by waves
we would cascade down
Rain is the verse of Creation
Longing the Holy Book of Creation

You, this kid, fleeing toward forty
What is it that gives rise to you?
What is it that you create?

      \*    \*    \*

She left secrets in the wind
     and so the heart was
     some time stone
     some time jasmine —
Is she the two poles
or are you? Answer me —
Oh, you're captivated,
     by the wind with the woman,
 by the tear with the laughter
     by the shadow and the brilliance of forty years
Is she the two poles?
Or a sparrow leaning against
     the limb of a question
How — dear God — and where?
This woman, forgiven her passions, left
     a waist, and two hands.

*Palestine Division May 1987*

# Echo

I remain the bird of promise no matter how long I'm gone
and you — when I spread my wings —
are the sky,
so don't ask me much,

                much,

as if I herd my madness

                before me

as if I herd the clouds.

## Assassination

The throne of the ode is a rose
who assassinates her maker
      and serves him so he grants her speech.
And if it is he she urges to go on he can get
to the farthest question like lightning broken
by the tale and the temptation
           and the shadows.
Hurl a lightning bolt
and he can get the prophecy — all of it —
from the embers of the vision
        to the woman of clouds.

*Tadmor Prison 1991*

# Diagnosis

The lover has half a heart
because he dedicated the other half
to love.
The executioner has two —
the first:
        to hate others until the end
and the second:
        to hate himself until the end
when he happens to tire from time to time
and is forced to toil
on behalf of one.

*Saydnaya Prison 1993*

# Prayer Niche of Wisdom

The trees
>are the forest's questions
>and you are my questions.
>You loved me — answer of the tree,
>>the first
>and I loved you — secret of the tree,
>>the last
and then kiss after kiss
>it began to ascend
>>the prayer niche of wisdom.

*Saydnaya Prison 1993*

## As Long As You Are, I Am

You can come in
without permission
and leave without permission
as long as my heart is open

        And I can be your confession
as long as you are my forgiveness
Your question
still my answer
Your rains
still my lightning
Your time
still my place —
So do I have to apologize
if my fate is surrounded
                    by obscurity
and my life encircled
                in poetry?

*Saydnaya Prison 1993*

## Teardrop

A tear can
    be a stone
    and be a rose —
Tell them:
You and I — we've been witness
since a long lament.

*March 1993*

# Dictation Lesson

Because she
writes me with her eyes
        I, when she errs
                in dictation,
And especially in writing my *hamzat*,
                in the middle,
I lend her my heart
to erase…
        until we start again,
from the beginning of the line.

*1993*

# Revolution

Before my imprisonment
whenever we stayed up late I would say:
This is the night of my life.
And now...
whenever I stay up I say:
This is a lifetime of nights.
Oh god,
even the "s" of the plural!

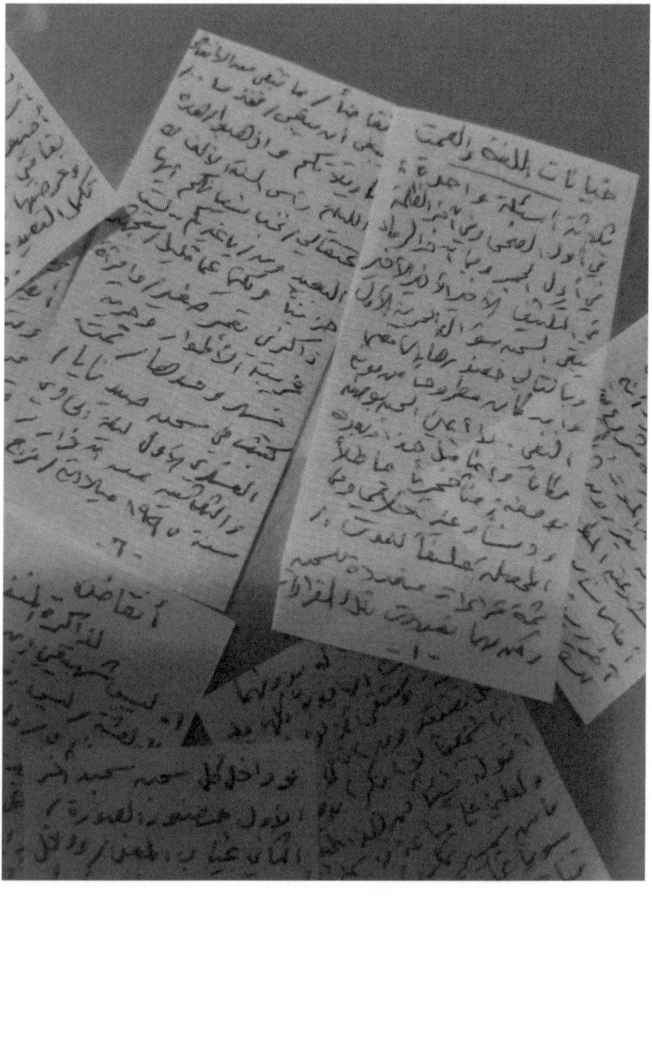

# An Interview with Faraj Bayrakdar

Conducted by Muhammad 'Ali al-Atassi
January 20th, 2002[1]

Q:  Faraj, you were born in 1951, and spent your childhood in the village of Tir Ma'ala, near Homs.  What does the village mean to you, and what was your life like in it?  Where did you complete your studies and when did your relationship with poetry and politics begin?

A:  The village, for me, its inhabitants and its character, is a symbol of the ultimate goodness, simplicity, and social solidarity that I am searching for.  I didn't sense the conservative nature of the village in [my] childhood.  During my youth, I began to raise existential questions and feel vast differences and some constraints.  But what protected me, in part, was the knowledge that I am a poet—this gave me a kind of sympathy, and even now, the village is requesting a pardon for me.

In the elementary and preparatory stages, I studied in the village, and in the secondary stage, I studied in Homs, and then at the university in Damascus.  Until the secondary stage, I was a member of the Ba'th Party, and then from the beginning of the seventies, my Marxist leanings began.  I

[1] Originally published in the cultural supplement of *al-Nahar*, a copy of the original Arabic of this interview can be found on *al-Hiwar al-Mutamaddin*: http://www.ahewar.org/debat/show.art.asp?aid=651&r=0

didn't announce my resignation from the Ba'th party until the mid-seventies when I was in Hungary where my Marxist direction became clear. At that time, I didn't know of the existence of an organization called the Communist Action League, but my knowledge of them began shortly after that. I started to perceive that I had an affiliation to communism, but I wanted to make my choice: Politburo, Bakdash, the League. The League was new, and I felt close to its tenets. I joined it in 1979 after finishing [my] military service.

In Damascus, I lived a life of displacement, especially in the phase of persecution between 1984 and 1987, when I was elected as a member of the politburo of the League. Damascus is a city that I was not comfortable with at all during every period of my residence there. I felt only the necessities of friendships, cultural movement, and political life in a capital that polarizes all currents. As a geography, an environment, and a structure, I felt Damascus pressing down on me, and my spirit confined by it.

I got married in 1979 to a friend in the party—a native of Dar'a—who came to study in Damascus, and I lived with her until 1986. She was arrested before me by eleven months in April 1986, and she remained in prison for four years. As for my daughter, she was born in 1983. During our first detention, my daughter was able to visit her mother while I was deprived of visits for five years. Then, my daughter's visits began after her mother got out of prison.

Q: In the mid-seventies, you, with a group of your friends,

published a literary journal; what was its name, who partici-
pated in it, and why did it stop?

A: This journal didn't have a title. We called it "The Liter-
ary Notebooks." It was published by a group of young writ-
ers at the university (I was studying Arabic literature), and we
distributed it to our friends. It specialized partially in poet-
ry and stories, but mostly consisted of subjects that are not
pulished in the official press. Because of it, I was detained for
three months in 1978. The young writers who published it
were: Jamil Hatmal, Riyad al-Salih al-Hussayn, Wa'il al-Sawwah,
Bashir al-Bakr, Ghassan 'Izzat, and Muwaffaq Sulayman.

Since 1976, poetry has become an essential choice in my
life. I published my first collection in 1979, but since my devo-
tion to political party work, in 1981, I stopped writing poetry
because of lack of time, [having] many political responsibil-
ities, and the moral and emotional duty towards my impris-
oned friends. I was no longer capable of "carrying two water-
melons" together, and I didn't come back to it until after my
detention when it was clear that I would not resume writing
poetry except in prison.

Q: And how did you "carry two watermelons" in prison, if
that can be said?

A: Poetry and politics are not incompatible, but poetry con-
flicts with direct, organizing work. The truth is that poetry is
the antithesis of prison, just as life is the opposite of death.

But one opposite transcends another and gives birth to it. The moment of writing is the moment of true freedom, and poetry is the vastest space of freedom without exception. Prison convenes the search for windows to freedom, and for me... the only way out before me was writing, as a form of combating captivity. The issue imposed itself on me beyond desire and intellectual calculation. Prison creates suffering; suffering provokes the mind and creates a specific atmosphere that pushes you to write about your sufferings in that it allows you to circumscribe it and then control it.

Q: But didn't you fear that the poetry would captivate, mold, and constrain your feelings? Were you afraid that your imprisonment would control your poetry in a trap [of] provocative and antagonistic directness, making it lose some of its aesthetic and literary equilibrium?

A: Poetry is democratic with its writer and reader. It never compromised my feelings; rather, it gave me a space for a surprising, extraordinary, and vast freedom. Poetry allowed me to control my prison, rather than my prison controlling me. Despite my belief that this peril is always the companion of the poet, it raises itself with greater insistence through the relationship of politics with poetry, which sometimes results in direct or provocative writings. In prison, this fear was present, and it wasn't voluntary; I tried not to fall into it depending on what my ability and potential allowed. I tried to be careful, and I think that what protected me, to a degree, is that I didn't write about aspects of the political struggle in prison. I would lean towards sentiment, memory, and transparent human issues that emerge from the feelings and suffering of the prisoner. I can say that I was imprisoned with what I felt at its moment; the revolution, the struggle, and everything else receded, and what remained was my longing for my mother, my daughter, my village, my friends. Prison raises these subjects, and they are distant from directness and do not lose their vitality. I tried to create artistic and symbolic equilibriums reflecting [my] condition without falling into directness. There are two terms, captivity and freedom, that I was never afraid of using directly. They enfold in themselves a charge that does not fade, not for the reader and not for the poet.

On the other hand, I can say that I did not write about my suffering only, but about the suffering of others around me, in all its human, living, and familial aspects. The tragedy of prison is not only reflected in the person of the incarcerated, but also in life outside of prison: many families have been destroyed and fallen apart, divorces, conditions of poverty and despair.

Q: Do you believe that what allowed you to endure in prison was your ideological conviction or was there also a human and emotional element?

A: I think what allowed me to endure in prison is a group of concepts that bring particular things to mind. For example, love is one of the components of resilience. Poetry too. Despair as well, but not in the sense of suicide or surrender and far from the despondency that means complete paralysis or apathy. In despair, I see an active strength; nothing other than this force was able to remove the walls of the place I was in. There is also sadness, not in the sense of anguish, but in the sense of grief that I feel as a profound value that has great provocation.

In addition to the concepts of love, poetry, despair, and sadness, there is also a moral dimension. For I, in my very constitution, am undefeatable, and consequently, the only option before me, is to remain steadfast. Suppose that I am not a communist, and that they arrested me and wanted to make me succumb. I feel that I am a man who is undefeatable and unyielding. At certain moments, I would question myself and wish that I was able to [succumb]! There are many who are able and content, but for me it was clear: my life wouldn't accept it. I am not bringing this up out of self-conceit but as a dilemma of mine. Luckily, I got out of prison despite this.

Q: From what you have said, can we say that human meanings and a moral system play a larger role than the ideological dimension in human resilience?

A: Exactly. Ideology does not protect someone from failure, destruction, and breakdown. What protected me was my respect for human existence and my trust in it generally, and my conviction that a human being as a value must not deviate or become corrupted. What protected me was my moral system and my conviction that I should not be permitted to disturb my mother's or daughter's feelings and that I should push them to not feel pity or sadness. What concerned me was that I fortify myself as a human being, even if I wasn't a member of the party. Self-invincibility and endurance are individual, and the ideological system does not protect anyone except in the conditions of a popular uprising.

Q: Do you think your resistance in prison was a defense of the party and its ideas or a defense of human values (although I am aware that the two are intertwined) and how do you explain your endurance after the fall of the Soviet Bloc?

A: I can say that I don't accept the oppression of anyone in any form or place or inside any regime. In an encounter with a security officer who came to meet with us at Tadmor Prison in order to find out if our "hot heads," as he believed, had cooled off in light of the conditions at Tadmor… this officer started to inform us of all the changes in the world and the fall of the socialist system. It was his belief that informing us of all of these developments was a guarantee of our submission, but my response to him was the following: has the Syrian regime changed or is it still a dictatorship? If the regime was still a dictatorship, then nothing had changed for me because I am not an adherent of the socialist system, and I have a lot of reservations about it, the most important of which is the absence of democracy. And until now, if nothing has changed, then I am not afraid to return to prison. In the end, what concerns me is that I am in harmony with my own convictions and my humanity.

Q: Did the breakdown of some people, the collaboration of others, and the slander affect you, and how did you live through it?

A: The issue was very painful for me—an agonizing bitterness—not from a political perspective, but from a human one. Let me say that I would have pity sometimes, in the sense that I felt a sadness towards these people, and this is one of the reasons for my continuous sorrow in prison because they were able to destroy part of a person, part of his physical, spiritual, and moral being. There is no one who breaks down because of his own will, and all who were weakened or recanted did so under enormous coercion and at a horrifying threshold of torture that is not easy to endure. It is a human issue, and in advance, I have pity for the person who is breaking down, and it is possible for me to stand by his side, care for him, and fortify him spiritually. Sometimes, close relations with him are generated, and I can understand the reason for his break down. I should not participate in destroying what human values remain in him. Whatever the case is, I am against the torturer and for the victim so long as he doesn't move to the side of the torturer. Who I don't sympathize with is the one who breaks down and turns into an informer.

Q: Faraj, could you tell us about the stages and places of your arrest?

A: In 1987, I was arrested in Damascus and imprisoned in

Palestine Division for interrogation. I remained in solitary for four months and spent most of those [months] under torture. In the end, we were able to shut down the 'dossier' of interrogation and cut the threads [leading to our comrades]. We were transferred from that division to another, much like a transfer station, and we stayed in that situation until we were transferred to one of the prisons. While we were there, a new wave of arrests was launched, and then papers were discovered, and other matters clarified that most of our previous confessions were false. In light of this, we were brought back to Palestine Division, and the interrogation began again, and we were subjected to it for another seven months. During this period, the interrogation sessions were every two days on average. After that, in February 1988, sixteen prisoners of our group, I among them, were transferred to Tadmor Prison. We stayed in Tadmor for four years, and from there we were transferred to Saydnaya Prison where I stayed until I was released.

Q: Did you reach a state of physical or psychological weakness during the period of interrogation? And for you, what were the most painful means of torture?

A: I wouldn't be exaggerating if I said that I wasn't alive in such a state. To me, what was important was enduring until I passed out. It would console me that they couldn't get anything [out of me]. After passing out, extracting a confession becomes impossible. As for them, they carefully studied the limit separating life and death, and they would try to stop before it by a little. For me, what they call the German chair, and what I call the Nazi chair, was the most intense means of torture in terms of causing pain, especially the subsequent consequences of back pain and temporary paralysis of the hands that lasted months, I was left on it one time for a period of two hours (the German chair consists of a metal chair that the prisoner is bound to and then the back of the chair is folded to the outside in the opposite direction such that it puts pressure on the prisoners back, arched to its extreme limit). When a prisoner is put on this chair and his back is pinched, the world (life and death) becomes, to him, half exhalation and half inhalation. A complete inhalation or a complete exhalation could kill him, and he must balance his breathing on the edge of pain between a partial exhalation and a partial inhalation. His life rests on that decisive thread.

Q: How did you return to poetry during this period after stopping for years?

A: After two weeks passed, it was as if the poetry emanated on its own as a defense mechanism. A verse came to my mind. I thought: how can I write it down without a pen and paper available! I said to myself that I would try to kill time by attempting to formulate short, intense verses to comfort myself. I composed, for example, a song for my mother and other simple things of that type. I felt that this was a very comforting mechanism, especially because the times I spent in my solitary cell outside of the interrogation periods, were long and boring. One time, they returned me to my cell, carrying me on a blanket, and all of a sudden, Malik Bin al-Rayb appeared to me when death was approaching him. I was half-comatose but at a peak moment of wakefulness, I sensed a resemblance between him and me. I wasn't fearful of death, only saddened. The introduction of what would become the poem "Vision" came to me:

> I was neither alive
> nor dead, so I made room for him
> Oh, how the tightness of the space shamed me.

I spent a week in my cell, exhausted and weary, mentally and spiritually, to such a degree that it wouldn't allow me to complete the poem. After that, I became able to walk a little, so I was moved to the infirmary for the injury of a broken rib. In the infirmary, the torture stopped and a period of convalescence passed, and I had some quiet days which allowed me to finish the poem.

Q: How did you write it? In your mind or on paper? And how long did it remain preserved in your mind before it found its way to paper, and did you alter it later?

A: In my mind, of course—my memory became trained once again in memorization even if this does not allow you to write long poems. Also, in Tadmor, there are no paper or pens, but I was able to train my memory more and depend on other comrades for memorizing some verses. Even then, I wasn't at ease, and I tried, on my own, to memorize all of the poems. As for the first time I wrote the poem "Vision" down on paper, it was in Tadmor, when they came to us with a pen to record our medication needs. I exploited the opportunity, and wrote it on cigarette paper. But it did not take long before I destroyed it because of the meticulous inspection we were subjected to each month. Later, our fear decreased and our expertise increased, and we invented ink from tea and onion peels and used it for writing by means of a wooden stick that we found in the courtyard. But the writing stayed at the level of a code; I would write the beginning of some verses that I was afraid of forgetting. The first time I wrote in the sense of real paper and pens, was in 1992 when we were transferred to Saydnaya Prison. I can say that "Vision" was preserved in my memory for five years, or until the end of my confinement at Tadmor. In truth, the number of poems I wrote during this period was small in comparison to what I wrote later in Saydnaya Prison. Often, I would avoid changing the poem so as to not distort [it in] my mind or weaken my memory.

Q: What was more difficult for you: the eleven months you spent under torture in Palestine Division or the five years you spent in Tadmor Prison?

A: Apart from the first weeks of the initial torture, necessarily savage in its power and force, apart from this type of torture, Palestine Division was easier than Tadmor, despite the fact that

it was underground, without sun or air. After the most danger-
ous part of the interrogation, you can feel a sort of reassur-
ance, even though at any time, you may have to "eat the tire"
(lashes or beatings on the body while confined from the neck
to the knees in the hole of a rubber tire). But to us, in the end,
the tire became a diversion especially in that there was the lure
of getting a cigarette from our comrades in the wake of each
tire [session.] Perhaps, it was because none of the comrades
broke during the period of interrogation, and they didn't feel
that the torturer was stronger than they were. Our being sent
to Tadmor, all of us, was disciplinary, a kind of revenge.

As for Tadmor, no...the entire situation was oppressive, wor-
rying, and terrifying. Tadmor is a kingdom of death and mad-
ness. The problem is not just what happens to you, but what
you see happening to others: the crushing or breaking or kill-
ing. For us, it was clear that our lives were not uselessly squan-
dered—only the beatings were present at every moment: when
food was brought, when leaving and returning from a break, at
roll call. In other words, they invent any way to beat you. If you
stand at attention, they ask you: "You '*akrut*, why are you stand-
ing at attention?" And then they assail you with punches and
kicks. If you stand at ease, it's the same case. Thus, you are not
safe, cut off and thrown into the desert, with no strength or pow-
er in you. Whereas in Palestine Division, you are in Damascus,
and perhaps you can smuggle in a piece of news or maybe you
scream a sound, and it is heard. But there, you scream into the
desert. Tadmor Prison is truly a disgrace in the history of Syria
and to all of humanity. This insane kingdom must be closed.

Q: Did you always hate your torturer, and didn't you sometimes ask yourself where the human being was inside the torturer?

A: In moments of torture, I would, at times, sympathize with some of the torturers. It was clear to me that he was forced to undertake a duty imposed on him beforehand, and no sooner would the officer be absent, than he would whisper a word in your ear or lessen the force of the beating. I used to differentiate between the torturers through their voices or their degree of force in using the instruments of torture. There are some torturers who do more than what is required of them, and I would hate them at the moment of torture, but after I returned to solitary, and I thought over and contemplated it, I would pity them because their humanity was eradicated, and they were transformed into the depraved. In the end, these are part of my people, and they destroy my people: they destroy the prisoner and the jailer as well as the citizen outside of the prison. Today, after my release, I can say that I do not despise any torturer who was one of the soldiers and non-commissioned officers; as for those amongst the officers, I also do not despise them, but I am offended by and feel contempt for a number of them, and I am not ready to engage with them.

Q: What was your relationship like with your body during the period of torture and did you have affection for it?

A: At moments, I would feel that the entity that was the most empathetic with me, the most intimate towards me, the most defensive of me, was my body. Luckily, my body never abandoned me, and consequently, periods of time passed in which I began to commiserate with it and apologize to it. In a way, I am also responsible for its torment. My love for my body was great, especially in the initial period of interrogation. It is my most loyal friend, and even while it complains to me sometimes, not to weaken or abandon me, but so that I commiserate with it—I felt towards it like the way Antara felt towards his horse.

Q: And what about your relationship to your prison cell?

A: Contrary to the alienation, pressure, and darkness that you imagine in the prison cell, I passed through periods in which I felt safety in my solitary cell while the danger was in the interrogation room. When I would go down into solitary, I felt as if I was returning to my mother's womb. Whenever its door was closed, I was safe. At moments, I would feel a longing and affection for it. At other moments, when my body wasn't in pain, I would grow weary of its smallness where the head is bent from the lowness of the ceiling and the legs are curled up because of its short length.

Q: What are the most painful, human moments that are still stuck in your mind from the period of interrogation?

A: Let me say that imprisonment is, on the whole, a continuous human moment. I can't summon all of its details, but let me say that hearing the voice of a woman subjected to torture creates a type of emotion that is impossible for a person to pass off in his life—seeing two people who are exhausted from torture, their feet are swollen, and they can't walk, but one's condition is slightly better than the other, so he tries to carry his friend even though he is unable to carry himself in the first place. Also, although one is not the real culprit, he volunteers to receive punishment in place of his comrade whose state of health makes him unable to endure anymore.

Q: Were you overcome by tears at times?

A: In truth, I was raised in a traditional way, and the subject of tears is a difficult one for men. I've remained this way for a long part of my life, but when the interrogation ended, and I had a clear conscience, I no longer feared that anyone of them would consider my tears a weakness. Just as others have related to me as a poet and have an understanding of this calling, the issue became easier for me, so I let myself go. Numerous scenes affected me and made me cry, and usually they didn't pertain to me personally but to the situation of others and their families. There were families with five brothers in detention, or you would hear about another prisoner who was allowed a visit after 18 years. They brought him out to see his family, and he didn't recognize his father or brother and wanted to go back from the mesh [grille]. The issue wasn't resolved until their cards were verified to confirm the identity of the visitors. Or another prisoner who went out for his first visit after dozens of years of detention and saw his family crying from behind the mesh. He called out: "Mama, why are you crying, Mama?" And then the woman's crying intensified. In the end, the lady says to him: "I'm your sister, your mother, may she rest in peace." In the face of stories like these, I can't bear it and I give myself over to tears.

Q: Did you cry from the intensity of the torture?

A: No, when confronting a torturer, I never felt I could cry, no matter how intense the pain—with the exception of electricity, which to me was the easiest of the forms of torture. But there is a point at which a person screams without any possibility of controlling the scream at all. In the "tire" or the "German chair," I could keep control of my screaming for a while. As for electricity, the screaming begins with the arrival of the first shock without one being conscious of oneself, and the pain ceases and stops immediately when the current stops whereas with the other means of torture, the pain and the scars remain. With electricity, I would ask myself when it had stopped, how did those sounds come out of me? It is an inverted scream and a howl—bestial sounds whose traits, between a cry for help and a wail, are unclear.

Q: Did you cry when you were face to face with your family?

A: When facing my parents, I never allowed myself to cry—no matter how intense the pain. My concern was to give them the impression that I was in control of my situation, holding up, and was comfortable, to fortify them as I fortified myself, in order to not let them grow weak. I didn't cry except for once in front of my younger brother, the one closest to me, who was a prisoner in Saydnaya with the same charge. Upon my arrival there, coming from Tadmor, I requested to be reunited [with him.] My longing for him was great, and to me, if I saw him, then it would be as if I had seen my entire family and reconnected with the outside world that I was cut off from. At the beginning, they agreed that I could see my brother in an outside room for five minutes while waiting for them to study my request. They brought him in, and I went out to see him with sixteen friends behind me. And as soon as we saw each other... we embraced freely, and for an instant I asked myself: "Do I give in or not?" And at the moment of the embrace, I heard from behind me the gasps and sobs of comrades, and as they began to reach me, I gave in. The second time that I cried in front of him was when the news of the death of my friend the writer, Jamil Hatmal, reached me. I could never control my emotions and I came out of our communal cell without being afraid of anyone hearing my cries.

Q: When was the first time you saw your one, young daughter after you entered prison?

A: I saw her for the first time through a photograph that came to me in Tadmor Prison. One of our fellow prisoners was allowed an exceptional visit during which his family gave him a group of various photos of the other comrades' families without names. When he returned to the barracks, the boys distributed the photos, and I was the only one who didn't receive one. A final picture of a young girl in a red dress, taken in a children's studio, remained without an owner. So through a type of deduction, my comrades called out and said it must be a picture of my daughter, Somar. I hesitated awhile as I looked at the picture, and in the beginning, I felt I didn't recognize her and kept scrutinizing her features. Does she look like me or her mother! Finally, my sight fixed on her eyes, and I sensed it was her; she began to move and twinkle, and in seconds, I no longer saw any features or clothes except the eyes saying: "I'm your daughter, I'm Somar." Then I felt a gleam of light. It really was her. I started jumping for joy and saying: "Hey, guys, it's Somar. It's really her." I remember that the others—tears came to their eyes, but as for me, no, because the sorrow diminished and changed to an overflowing joy beginning from the moment I recognized her.

The first time I saw her in reality was in Saydnaya Prison where they informed me of a visit. We agreed that we wanted the first visit privately in a room and not through the mesh, especially after all these years. I came out and my decision was final: either I would see and touch my daughter after six years or there was no need for a visit. After going back and forth with the administration, they permitted it. I came out and saw a little girl of nine years and guessed that she was my daughter even if, after all these years, she didn't resemble the little girl that I left behind. I approached her and picked her up asking: "How are you, Baba?" She answered: "Fine." I relaxed a little and asked her: "Do you recognize me? Tell me about some of our memories together." She answered: "One time, you took me to a lot of water (she remembered that I took her to a swimming pool), and another time, you took me to the see-saw and the trains going up and coming down (the amusement park)." With that, I became much more comfortable because in my daughter's mind, there were at least two scenes of us together. Today, after my release from prison, I asked her again about our memories together before my imprisonment, and I discovered that even those scenes have faded from her memory.

Q: If we go back to Tadmor Prison, it seems that your presence there coincided with the presence of another brother of yours who was accused of belonging to the Muslim Brotherhood, but you didn't know that until after you left Tadmor. What was the reason [for this], and can you describe the conditions of this prison as you lived [them]?

A: The reason is that the communal cells and the courtyards are completely separated, and even if it happened that I did run into him, I don't believe I would have been able to recognize him because all of the prisoners have their heads and mustaches shaved, their clothes are all the same, and they are forced to walk outside of the communal cells with their heads bent down. They come out of the cells like a frenzied herd, as if there is a poisonous viper or predatory wolf inside, and it's the same situation when they return to it, where everyone wants to be the first entering or leaving in order to avoid the lashes of the whips and the cables that await them at the door of the blocks whether they are coming in or going out. It's heinous how one's sense of life takes over because out of the sweetness of the spirit, you find that each one throws himself towards the front. The sounds of their steps as they come and go resemble the sound and roar of the hooves of a herd. Pushing each other, seventy or eighty prisoners pouring out of the gate of the communal cell in seconds, and then the sergeant would come and ask calling out the number of the communal cell, "How long has it been for you, Number 17?" and the head of the block must respond to him, "We've been out an hour, sir." If not, a beating is the fate of the entire communal cell.

As a result of this state, the break is like a collective punishment, and I called it a 'cutting off of breath' instead of a break. The first time, they took us out into the yard barefoot, and they ordered us to walk around with our eyes closed and our heads bowed, alongside the wall, circling around the yard. They concocted anything to beat us, and from there, they took us back to the communal cells. Thus, tragic incidents would [cause] horrendous laughter to erupt, and we would try to calm each other down because if our laughter was heard, we would be exposed to a beating again. Even then, we couldn't resist our laughter, especially when we were subjected to a round of collective beatings. A half-hysterical laughter.

We would seek out any pretext for a hunger strike in order to improve the conditions of our detention and found no better pretext than refusing to go out into the yard for a break. A break in Tadmor is obligatory for the prisoner and not a right. As a punishment, we were subjected to a round of collective beatings, and after that, the hunger strike was announced. The strike lasted one day, and we ended it after we obtained a promise for improved conditions and to stop the random beatings and insults. But nothing changed, a year and a half passed, and in the end, we despaired of any attempt to improve our situation. After we were convinced that our blood wasn't squandered, we had a strike for a second time, and it lasted 11 days. In the end, we achieved some gains that would be rescinded.

Q: Did you write your poem entitled "Hunger Strike" during that period?

A: Yes, the entire communal cell was on strike, and our demands were simple: Stop the beatings, stop the insults, a newspaper, a book, papers, and pens, a special yard for the break without the presence of soldiers. We added a radio and visitation rights with the certainty that both would be difficult to achieve. The goal was to obtain the largest amount of our demands. In the beginning, by means of torture, they tried to dissuade us from continuing the strike, but after several days, the beatings began to form a threat to our lives. In reality, our response was suicidal, and we started banging on the door, shouting: "Down with dictatorship! Long live freedom!" In the end, the administration was disconcerted and responded to a reasonable part of our demands—a yard, a newspaper in intermittent form, stopping the beatings, some books from the prison library, and we agreed to break up the strike.

Before that strike, we only studied it theoretically. We knew that a person can endure approximately a whole month without damaging his body. But I was surprised that apprehensions about a strike are always greater than its implementation. In the first four days, I was able to walk, but on the fifth day, I began to weaken. We started to reduce our movement to conserve calories. After the first four days, the stomach presses in on itself and makes due with itself. Consequently, what surpasses the hunger that oppresses a person is the sense of time. After several days pass, the oppression of time is more intense than anything else—stone time, a day seemed to be a year. You put your heavy head on the blanket, and you feel like it's a rock. On the ninth day, I started to sense clearly the emaciation and leanness of everyone's form, and I composed the poem.

Q: You spent the last 9 years of your detention in Saydnaya Prison. What was the situation like there?

A: The conditions in Saydnaya prison are altogether preferable to the stages we passed through in the rest of the prison camps. Even then, in the first two years, our situation was worse than the rest of the groups since we were subjected to routine searches and everything was confiscated from us: the radio, the table, the small lamp, the 'oud hand-made from the wood of fruit boxes and thread from nylon socks. After three years, the situation began to improve, and in the final two years, a limited human relationship was created with the guards; we were permitted books and radios, and the[ir] dealings with us were comfortable to an extent. Although I don't wish to say that any prison is comfortable, the general condition, in its entirety, changed in Syria in the latter period as a result of external and internal pressure pertaining to human rights.

For me personally, the first three years in Saydnaya were extremely bad, health-wise and psychologically. I had developed heart problems as a result of the conditions of pressure: my family, my daughter, my wife's difficult state after her release from prison. It was a great gulp of pain that I couldn't swallow with ease. Even then, I would resist it by way of an abundance of writing that was like a restoration of balance and emptying my "quiver " under the anxiety of death. After these three years passed, my zeal lessened and poetic writing came and went depending on my emotional and psychological state.

Q: In what form were women present with you in prison?

A: An expression of the South African poet Breyten Breytenbach comes to mind here: "the woman is everything that a prisoner seeks and that he can never find." Women are the freedom lost in prison. Her presence is overwhelming and takes forms that didn't come to my mind previously to the extent that I imagined in one of the poems that a friend says to me: "How beautiful would God be, if he were a woman." And I respond to him, pointing out: "What is God, then?" If it were otherwise, then it would be a tragedy. Let me say that in prison, women took on a sacred dimension, sometimes as a god, and sometimes as a saint. The visit in which there were women (mother, sister, daughter, wife) was really exceptional, and the prisoner who is visited and his visit lacks women—there is a sort of grief in it. The existence of women is distant from the body and becomes abstract, taking on a phantom form in the imagination of the prisoner.

To me, in prison, the aspect of the woman most missed is her voice and shadows, something close to an apparition, separated from its earthliness, a Sufi state. In Tadmor, the presence of women takes the forms of the nurse, the mother, the saint who takes care of you. In Saydnaya, the situation is a lot less bad, and the presence of women takes on different dimensions.

Q: Do you remember your first encounter with a woman's voice after the five years of your imprisonment in Tadmor?

A: In Saydnaya, a small, one-wave radio was smuggled in for us, and we were astonished by a female voice that we didn't know repeating the song, "Words" two or three times a day. I began to float in the spaces and expanses of that voice, and I really felt that confinement had become easier to bear.

Months later, we met the old prisoners, and the first question we asked them was: "who is the owner of that beautiful voice, the one who sings Nizar Qabbani's poem "Words," and I was told it was the Lebanese singer Majda al-Rumy.

Q: Do you remember when you saw your poems written down on paper for the first time, and what were your feelings like at that moment?

A: Yes, immediately after our arrival at Saydnaya Prison, old comrades in prison were able to smuggle paper and pens to us. I poured out the poems onto paper right away, with the help of two of my friends who had memorized parts of the poetry I had composed in Tadmor Prison. After that, we smuggled the poems that I had written to another communal cell and from there, out of the prison. When the matter was completed, I felt as if this great concern had been removed from my shoulders, even to the point that my memory began to forget what I had memorized, as if what I had written was transferred from the private to the public. My attachment to it abated, and my position towards it became more objective. It was a moment of exceptional happiness; the elements of my resistance and equilibrium were restored with a greater strength, and my faith in poetry and its role was fortified, especially after positive reactions arrived from outside.

Q: During the period of your detention, your collection *A Dove in Free Flight* was published, and it contains some of your poems written in prison. It is said that the publication occurred without your knowledge; what was your position when you learned the news? Did you change your opinion after the positive reactions that the collection met all over the world, after it was translated into a number of foreign languages and the international campaign for your release began?

A: In the beginning, I was very upset for several reasons; first of all, I didn't choose the poems that were included in the collection, and some of them were still in the stage of their first draft. There was also a danger that once again, I would be deprived of paper and pen, and I hadn't written down everything that was in my "quiver." At that time, I was contending with feelings of the futility of poetry in the face of prose in reaching the broadest classes of people and moving the situation. For this reason, I wasn't afraid when I wrote my defense in front of the State Security Court, which was considered suicidal by some. I wrote it with all of my convictions and feelings in the hope that it would induce a response about the general situation and that every citizen would understand it. As for the poetry, I would ask myself who would read and empathize with it. I wasn't aware that it could provoke all these reverberations. But after the first positive reactions reached [me], I realized I was wrong and, once again, my faith in the status and role of poetry was strengthened, and I became more obstinate and happy even if the price was a delay in my release from prison.

Q: Didn't you ask yourself if the positive reception of your collection is linked to its artistic merit or to its writer being a prisoner of conscience?

A: Let me say that the issue doesn't worry me a great deal because I don't consider myself a great poet—these are my artistic competencies and potentialities. I don't wish anyone to exaggerate or underestimate them. As for the positive reactions, I believe that they were exaggerated, and that doesn't relate to its aesthetic or artistic aspect, but rather to people's desire to be in solidarity with a case that has a human dimension, especially in that the meaning in it is that a poet is imprisoned.

Q: Did you read other poets in Saydnaya Prison, and who was the poet whose poems you missed reading the most?

A: I read all the poetry that fell into my hands. The poet whose new work I missed reading the most was Mahmoud Darwish. For example, in the newspapers, I read about his collection, *Why Did You Leave the Horse Alone*, and I kept waiting for three years before I could obtain it. Mahmoud Darwish is an inexhaustible poet, and he is always able to renew himself. In my entire life, I have never read poetry that enters into my interior and affects me emotionally like Darwish's poetry with its images, content, warmth, simplicity, structure, and complexity. Contrary to what usually happens, I always search for echoes of myself in his writings. In his poetry, I seek out my childhood and the stations of my life. When he speaks about the dove, I remember the doves' nests in our village, and my feelings when it flies, the wind and its relationship to the trees, my relationship with my mother, freedom.

Reading poetry is joy mixed with a beautiful exhaustion, like the state of someone coming out of a beautiful, sexual encounter. At the end of the reading, I light a cigarette and float in a sea of emotions.

Q: Can you describe for us your feelings on the day of your release, and what was the reception of you from your family and daughter like?

A: I profess that I left with [a sense] of agony, since it was my dream that all of us leave prison without looking back, and it wasn't fulfilled. We left prison, and some of our comrades were still in it. We emerged to freedom while bidding farewell to those who remained in captivity. Because of this, I didn't go to meet my family in the village, but went to visit the families of those who remained in Saydnaya.

We were transferred by bus to Damascus, and in the beginning, I didn't recognize any one of its streets, tunnels, bridges, and sites that were totally new to me. I couldn't figure out our direction until we arrived at a point that I knew from a long time ago.

I spent a day in Damascus, and the next day, I headed to Homs where my family was waiting for me in the area of the bus station. As I got off the bus, the first to greet me was the face of my daughter, and I felt like my power was weakening and I feared that I wouldn't reach her...I reached her, leaned on her for a while, and embraced her for an extended time and cried. After that, I no longer saw anyone: hugs and kisses as I was swimming among family and friends.

Q: Don't you feel pangs of remorse towards her because of the suffering that she went through?

A: I never feel that, and luckily, she put me at ease with her maturity and comprehension of my circumstances and position. She considers herself my partner; just as I paid a price not for my own sake, but for the sake of my family, people, and nation, so did she. Luckily, during the period of my absence, she chose for herself a mother and father in every meaning of the word—my brother and his wife. And she calls them "Mom" and "Dad." Today, I am an additional father, less important than my brother, like as if I am a friend of hers.

Q: Today, after getting out of prison, do you have any desire to return to political and party work?

A: Before my detention, I used to say that it was enough that I undertake my party work completely, to endure its responsibilities to the end and be detained, and then I will return as a poet in prison. I was and still am a poet and the future of my life is with poetry. I am not an organizer; yes, I was and still am political and will continue to be interested in politics in its widest sense. And I will remain completely free to give my positions and convictions to whoever sees it as truly serving my people's cause. But as to my returning as an organizer in a narrow sense, no, because that is not in my nature. I was obliged to do it, there was no other choice, so I put aside the poet inside me under the pressure of responsibility and loyalty to friends and comrades.

Q: Is there a place for hatred in your heart, and can you turn the page of the past in light of the positive developments happening in Syria today [2002]?

A: In prison, I learned to believe in the human being in his sublime image, and consequently, hatred is out of the question for me because the human being who hates concedes a portion of his true humanity. Reconciliation is an issue that I cannot plunge into today as I am in need of time to observe the movement of reality and society and form a particular picture. However, I can say that I have hope that the regime will reconcile with society, even if it would necessitate many steps and large sacrifices from all sides, including from us. Turning the page is not like God forgiving what has happened; instead, there are conditions, the most important of which are the treatment of all that has occurred in the past, like the cases of the disappeared, for example. Then, all sides of the regime and political currents must participate in treating the wounds, creating particular reconciliations, and in recohering social and national concerns.

Q:  In conclusion, I would like to recall some of the verses of your poems in the light of the present:

> With thorns the guard caresses
> Your sparrows
> and the state bestows upon you
> a precautionary death

Today, who caresses your wounds, and what could be bestowed upon you aside from a "precautionary death"?

A:  There are hundreds of people, some of whom I know and others I don't, from Syria and all of the corners of the world, who have become like family to me.  There are also my parents, friends, and the sons of my village.  All of these people granted me, in place of a precautionary death, a precautionary freedom that I was afraid I would not obtain.

Q:          I was neither alive
            nor dead, so I made room for him
            Oh, how the tightness of the space shamed me

Where are you today, between life and death?  And has the place opened up on its horizons?

A:  I believe that I came out of this state several years ago, and that I am always on the endless shores of life and horizons and at horizons that do not end.

Q:           My cell is my body
             And the ode incidental freedom

What did you leave behind you in your cell after your body
had left it?

A:  I left behind some of the wreckage of my body, and yet I
restored it later on.  And I left a number of memories—I be-
lieve that they are rubble now.

Q:  Two fugitive gazelles: the wife and the daughter, how are
they today?

A:  They weren't accustomed to being fugitives. Yet, the for-
mer fell into the net of a raging oppression that led to her
illness, and the second has not yet found a suitable plain for
herself.  I hope to fashion a plain for her.

Q:              Nor are the poets like me when they mourn

A:  The pre-Islamic poets used to weep over the ruins of plac-
es and their longing for them.  I, like them, cry over ruins, but
the tragedy is that the ruins for us are human ruins, and they
have a greater impact and bitterness.  I know mothers, wives,
and siblings who have become human ruins.

Q:           I am calling
             I am not searching for a collective grave

just my country

Faraj, have you found your country?

A:  No, even now I have not found it.  I entered prison and Syria was a mass grave to me.  Now, has it remained like that? The truth is that I don't know!  I have hopes, I have hopes, yet I am not certain.

Q:  You introduced your collection with the expression: "The freedom within us is greater than the prisons that we are in." Faraj, today, where is our freedom and where are our prisons?

A:  The freedom within me is still the stronger. Yet, it is upheld now by an additional freedom that others have granted me, and I am grateful to them all.  And if some of the phenomena of tyranny are still standing, my confidence is great that they will cease to exist, and I see some positive initiatives in this direction, but they are not exactly enough.  For example, the Emergency Law has not yet been abolished, and we could simply be returned to prison.

*Interview by Mohammed 'Ali al-Atassi*
*Translated by Shareah Taleghani*

# Coda

Afterword by Author

The poems of this collection were smuggled out of prison, written on cigarette paper. They were published in 1997, two years after they were smuggled out. And this was against my wishes. I was not thinking about publishing while I was shackled by detention. I enjoined those who smuggled them out to preserve them until I was released and not to let anyone look at them, unless my life came to an end in prison. I knew nothing of the mode and manner of the publication of this collection—neither while I was in prison nor after my release. Until a friend explained to me, more than ten years after the publication of the collection, that with another friend's cooperation, they were able to photocopy the poems that they read at the home of one of my family members. Then, they brought them to friends of mine in Paris, and they published them. Now, I'm indebted to all of them, despite the fact that my decision, at that time, was against publishing any of my writings, out of fear that the authorities would punish me by prohibiting visitations from my family. Yet, the results came out the opposite of what I had feared and expected. For the publication of the collection, and its translation into French, aided in widening the scope of the international campaign demanding my release. The first edition of this poetic collection came full of errors, gaps, and defects. This was due to the lack of clarity of some of the letters on the cigarette papers, and also because of my absence. In addition, the poem "Alphabetical Formation" was published before its completion in its final form, other poems came out without titles, and three short poems were missing. A friend, the Moroccan poet Abdellatif Laâbi, translated this collection into French under the title *Neither Alive, Nor Dead*. It was published by Dante Editions, with the first edition in 1997 and the second edition in 2012. The launch of the Syrian Revolution in March 2011 was the primary reason for the second edition, and also for the issuing of the second and third editions of my book that speaks about my experience in the prisons of the Syrian intelligence agencies for a period of fourteen years, *The Betrayals of Language and Silence.*

In prison, poetry was, for me, the most beautiful bird of freedom, and it is the most extreme exercise of freedom.

Now, I mean after the revolution of Syrians, poetry has become a bird with shattered wings, broken and sorrowful, as it sees, for the first time, in one place or country, Russian and American military bases and airports.

Outside of this Syrian exception, you would not find a Russian base where there is an American base, and the opposite is true.

Why is it that this exception has not happened anywhere but Syria?

It is not in the capacity of poetry to answer. Its capacity is only to leave, as a ruptured response, its wounds, facing this cursed world.

*Faraj Bayrakdar*
*Stockholm, February 5, 2020*

*Translated by Shareah Taleghani*

# Acknowledgements

In the strange genre of collaborative acknowledgements, as co-editors, we thank many of the same people, but each with our own emphasis, even at the risk of redundancy. First, were it not for Elias Khoury, this translation would never have come into being. As Shareah notes, Elias's seminars at New York University and his writings introduced her to worlds of texts, transformed the way she thinks about the connections between literature and politics, and inspired not only this translation and others, but her dissertation and first book. In addressing him directly, she writes: Elias, I am profoundly grateful for your teachings, wisdom, encouragement, and kindness. And Ammiel adds profound thanks to Elias for his courage, brilliance, unstoppable irreverence, and, most of all, his true and continuing friendship.

To Sinan Antoon, Rebecca Johnson, Jeff Sacks, and Tsolin Nalbantian, our wonderful collaborators, our gratitude to you all for your patience and the poignancy, deftness, and creativity of your translations. So many years later, we are truly thankful to have been able to learn from and work with you, and we watch your continuing and significant accomplishments in so many different fields with an abundance of good feeling. Shareah would also like to thank Leena Dallasheh for her help and for always being a sounding board over many years in all of her translation endeavors.

We both owe great thanks to the editors at journals and

venues whose initial excitement over Faraj's work allowed at least some of it to reach readers early on: many thanks to the editors at BOMB and Words Without Borders. We owe special thanks to Margaret Obank and Samuel Shimon, founders and editors of the extraordinary journal Banipal, dedicated wholly to translations of Arabic literature. Finally, we owe a debt of gratitude to the late Fred Dewey, then at Beyond Baroque in Los Angeles, who had planned to publish the book before running into insurmountable obstacles, but still published excerpts in Beyond Baroque magazine. After numerous attempts with many publishers over the years, Ammiel kept at it, refusing to believe that a text as important as this could go unrecognized. Words can hardly suffice to express our joy when Robert Booras and Zohra Saed expressed their immediate enthusiasm, and we give our heartfelt thanks to them and UpSet Press for seeing the importance of this collection and giving us the opportunity to publish it.

Over the years, Ammiel has watched Shareah's thought and work develop, from her time as a graduate student to the point of becoming colleagues at Queens College and the Graduate Center, CUNY. As Ammiel puts it, our connection over the years, and this truly collaborative work, done at such a pivotal historical moment, truly remains one of the great markers along my creative and intellectual journey, and I thank Shareah for continuing to share her rare and uncompromising perspective. And Shareah writes: to Ammiel, thank you simply for being you. When we first met back in 2002, I didn't really think of myself as a translator. It was your idea for this project, your gentle encouragement of all of us in translating this collection as well as poems for the 2003 public reading "Nothing but Iraq," that started me, like so many others, on the path of translation. I have learned so much from you in this process and so appreciate your support, thoughtfulness, and dialoguing over so many years.

Finally, to Faraj, for the poignancy and the unabating power of your words, our utmost gratitude and appreciation. While Ammiel and Faraj have never met, the sense we all feel in this common endeavor leaps out at Faraj's words when we gave him news of the publication: "I would like to thank all of you by my eyes, my hands, and my heart." As Shareah writes, thank you, Faraj, for your forbearance with the long wait to see this translation through, and, for that visit in Syria years ago where you and your daughter Somar generously welcomed me to your home, and for your constant willingness to deal with the trials, errors, and minutiae of translation. You forever remind us to look to the possibility of a just horizon. May you come to Homs in a little while.

# Biographical Notes

Winner of the 1998 Hellman-Hammet Award and 1999 Pen America Prize, **Faraj Bayrakdar** was born in 1951 in Tir Ma'ala, a village near Homs in central Syria. He began publishing poetry while still in high school. At the University of Damascus, he and a group of friends started a literary journal but texts in it led to his arrest and imprisonment for three months. His first collection, *You Are Not Alone*, came out in 1979, and was quickly followed by two more. He stopped writing in the early 1980s due to commitments in the Syrian Communist Action Party; his wife, also a party member, was arrested and spent four years in prison. In 1987, Bayrakdar was arrested again and remained in prison without trial until 1993 when he was sentenced to fifteen years hard labor for belonging to an unauthorized political organization. His imprisonment lasted more than twelve years, in three different prisons (Palestine Division, Tadmor, and Saydnaya). Throughout his detention he composed poetry, either from memory or using the most rudimentary tools. Without his knowledge, a group of friends in Beirut published *A Dove in Free Flight*, from which the poems here have been selected. The book was used, Elias Khoury writes, as "one of the instruments of pressure on the Syrian authorities to mobilize international, intellectual opinion, particularly in France, in order to set the poet free." After an international campaign on his behalf, Bayrakdar was released from prison during the brief political respite known as

"Damascus Spring" in 2000. In 2005, he left Syria and currently resides in Sweden. The Italian translation of *A Dove in Free Flight* won the 2017 Vercelli Festival Award and a corrected second edition of the original Arabic was published in 2020.

**Elias Khoury** was born in Beirut, where he now lives. Indelibly marked by his deep involvement in the Palestinian cause, Khoury has been consistently outspoken in fighting for freedom of expression and defending the rights of suppressed activists, thinkers, and writers. While he has won many prizes and awards and his works have been translated into many languages, he considers his greatest public honor the gesture made by a group of displaced Palestinians, when they named a tent city, erected in protest of Israeli settlements, after Khoury's fictional village in his novel *Gate of the Sun*. Author of thirteen novels, four volumes of literary criticism, and three plays, Khoury's work has always explored the exchange between fictional representation and events in the world. A major international author whose importance and stature only grows, Khoury has been Global Distinguished Professor of Middle Eastern and Arabic Studies at New York University, and taught at Columbia University, the Lebanese University, the American University of Beirut, and the Lebanese American University.

Poet, novelist, translator, critic, and scholar **Ammiel Alcalay** teaches at Queens College and The Graduate Center, the City University of New York. His books include *After Jews and Arabs*; *Memories of Our Future*; *Islanders*; *neither wit nor* *gold: from then*; *from the warring factions*, and *a little history*. He was given a 2017 American Book Award from The Before Columbus Foundation for his work as founder and General Editor of *Lost & Found: The CUNY Poetics Document Initiative* (lostandfoundbooks.org).

**Sinan Antoon** is a poet, novelist, scholar, and translator, and Associate Professor at New York University. Born in Baghdad, he left Iraq after the Gulf War. His books include the novels *I'jaam: An Iraqi Rhapsody*, *The Corpse Washer*, *Baghdad Eucharist*, and *The Book of Collateral Damage*, numerous collections of poetry, and various scholarly texts on classical Arabic poetry and poetics. His award-winning works have been translated into thirteen languages.

**Rebecca C. Johnson** is Associate Professor of English and the Humanities at Northwestern University. She is the author of *Stranger Fictions: A History of the Novel in Arabic Translation* and the translator, with the author, of Sinan Antoon's *I'jaam: An Iraqi Rhapsody*.

**Tsolin Nalbantian** is University Lecturer of Modern Middle Eastern History at Leiden University, The Netherlands. Her publications include *Armenians Beyond Diaspora: Making Lebanon Their Own*, and "Going Beyond Overlooked Populations in Lebanese Historiography: The Armenian Case." She is presently co-editing *Practicing Sectarianism* and *Diaspora and 'Stateless Power': Social*

*Discipline and Identity Formation.*

**Jeff Sacks** is Associate Professor and Chair of Comparative Literature at the University of California Riverside. His books include the award-winning *Iterations of Loss: Mutilation and Aesthetic Form, al-Shidyaq to Darwish*, and a translation of Mahmoud Darwish's *Why Did You Leave the Horse Alone*?

**R. Shareah Taleghani** is Assistant Professor and Director of Middle East studies at Queens College, the City University of New York. She is the author of *Readings in Syrian Prison Literature: the Poetics of Human Rights* and co-editor of *Generations of Dissent: Intellectuals, Cultural Production, and the State in the Middle East and North Africa.*

## Other Upset Press Titles

*a little history*, Ammiel Alcalay *(with re: public)*

*A Nuclear Family*, April Heck

*Beige*, Bruna Mori, George Porcari

*Born Palestinian, Born Black*, Suheir Hammad

*City of Pearls*, Sham-e-Ali Nayeem

*Desire of the Moth*, Champa Bilwakesh

*Drive-by Cannibalism in the Baroque Tradition*, Amir Parsa

*from the warring factions*, Ammiel Alcalay *(with re: public)*

*Hail*, Matthew Rotando

*Halal Pork & Other Stories*, Cihan Kaan

*Mediterranean*, Edited by Bhakti Shringarpure, Michael Busch, Michael Bronner, Versuka Cantelli, Melissa Smyth, Jessica Rohan, Gareth Davies, Jason Huettner, Noam Scheindlin *(with Warscapes Magazine)*

*Quiet of Chorus*, Vanessa Huang

*Slippers for Elsewhere*, Matthew Burgess

*The Blond Texts and the Age of Embers*, Nadia Tuéni

*The Comeback's Exoskeleton*, Matthew Rotando

*The Complete NothingDoings: In Which Is Elaborated a Wonderous Liberation Epistemopoetology (of Sorts)*, Amir Parsa

*The Ground Below Zero: 9/11 to Burning Man, New Orleans to Darfur, Haiti to Occupy Wall Street*, Nicholas Powers

*The Infected Nucleus*, Daniel Cordani, Robert Booras

*The New Night of Always*, Robert Booras

*Theater of War: The Plot Against the American Mind*, Nicholas Powers

*Tractatüus Philosophiká-Poeticüus*, Amir Parsa

*Vocalises*, Jenny Husk

### Forthcoming

*Insurgent Feminisms: Women Write War*, Edited by Bhakti Shringarpure, Versuka Cantelli

*Thirst*, Nicholas Powers